LIFE

IS A

JOURNEY

REV. MICHAEL PEYNADO

ISBN 978-1-0980-2715-5 (paperback)
ISBN 978-1-0980-2717-9 (hardcover)
ISBN 978-1-0980-2716-2 (digital)

Christian Faith Publishing, Inc.
832 Park Avenue
Meadville, PA 16335
www.christianfaithpublishing.com

The following Bible translations have been used in this volume: NIV: *New International Version*; KJV: *King James Version*; NKJV: King James Version; TCRB: *Thompson Chain Reference Bible*.

Printed in the United States of America

To the Westbury Divine Church of God Family and my dearest wife Nomey Peynado of fifty-three years.

She have weathered the storms of life with me in the good times and bad times.

She is my best friend.

CONTENTS

FOREWORD

Michael Peynado grew up in Jamaica at a time when the Drifters popular hit songs Sand in My Shoes, and Under the Boardwalk were at the top of the charts. Instead of being influenced to stay in a tourist culture of sand, sea, and sun, he embarked on a mission to industrial lands.

He journeyed only with his mother's mantra: "Trust God;" unaware as to where life would lead, and what success would look like.

It is a fascinating read, following his path, sharing the various turning points in his life and discovering lessons learned. God is always pleased with storied lives of faith patterned after Hall of Faith stories recorded in Hebrews 11.

As a young minister in the early 90's my first encounter with Michael was as my superior, Vice President of the Church of God in the Eastern New York district of churches. My first impression was how elegantly he dressed, exactly what caught his wife's eye when she first saw him at church. I learned he was an excellent tailor by trade, and unlike other tradesmen fixed himself and family first before trying to fix others, a principle of integrity embodied in his life and ministry.

The measure of his maturity, emotional security and success as a leader is evident in how he like Moses with Joshua, Naomi with Ruth encouraged, trained, supported, and respected my rise, along with other young men and women to leadership.

Subsequently he humbly accepted reverse mentoring—the younger teaching and leading the elder—during my tenure as President of the Assembly and Dean of our Christian Bible School. My prayer is that other pastors learn from Michael whose legacy will continue in a succession of leaders, and in his life story recorded in this book.

—Rev. Dr. Jefferson Bannister DMin, Drew University

Time change, but God's principles for growth and development of his people is alive today with power as when first written centuries ago. My husband Michael, fondly called "Mike" was the Phantom of my delight, when first he gleaned upon my sight. The imagery was in my mind, but my godly upbringing challenged me to remain low keyed and cautious.

Founding members Adam
and Hortense Dawkins

I was in nursing school at the time and he asked me to marry him. I told him when I graduate, I would. Upon graduation I did, and we have been married now for fifty two years. He has proven to be an excellent husband and an excellent father to our children.

He has demonstrated love and concern for people, good social skills, love, and a caring and sharing pastor. This book merged from his childhood experiences, that every child is precious and can be taught, if given the right opportunity. It is also to motivate adult teachers and parents not to give up on a child. It teaches one that he/

she can succeed in life, no matter what the circumstances may be, with faith in God all things are possible.

This, Book "Life is a Journey," is fitting to be read by any-one looking to be inspired and motivated in their quest for self-advancement. I truly believe that all those who read this book will find it to be very uplifting, resourceful and challenging, and will banish fear from the faint hearted.

—Nomey Peynado
Registered Nurse

Imagine my delight when asked by Pastor Michael Peynado to write a foreword for this book, and it was my pleasure to accept the challenge.

There is no doubt in my mind that for the author, "Life is a Journey" was a labor of love. As the title says, life is a journey for all of us and we know that nature compels us to move through this life from beginning to end.

Anyone meeting Pastor Michael Peynado in person for the first time, as I did many years ago, immediately recognizes his gentleness of spirit and his humility, and that spirit transcends in the pages of this book. This book unveils an amazing story of humble beginning, God first, faith, trust, reliance solely on God's direction, obedience and perseverance and the ultimate successes that were experienced from it all, and that you too as the reader will soon experience vicariously as you read his story, whether you are young or old.

Among the many revelations that this book holds, is one of his total surrender to God every step of the way, and one that you too can emulate in your life's journey.

His passion and zest for life encompasses a desire to bring change to the lives of others, and his ability to stir your emotions through touching your lives. My vision is that once you read this book, it will be an eye-opener to all the blessings that God has in store for you, if you just tap into it.

May we all be strengthened by the words from these pages, knowing God orchestrated this writing through his obedient manservant?

Hyacinth D. McKen,
Emeritus Senior Court Reporter at
Supreme Court of King's County, New York
May 15, 2019

I am honored to have been asked by Pastor Michael Peynado to do a "Foreword" for his book Life Is A Journey. For someone to put into words his reflections on his own life journey is indeed an accomplishment. Even more, I consider it an expression of thanks for the gifts that God has bestowed upon him and his humble offer of those gifts back to God. In every sentence, Pastor Peynado demonstrates his thankfulness to the mighty God that he serves. It is also a gift to his family, and especially his succeeding generations. Through his sharing, they will better know the contours and even detours of his life and understand them as steppingstones to be built upon. The late anthropologist Margaret Mead once declared that "too many stories go silently into the grave."[1] Not so the Michael Peynado story. Hopefully, others might heed Mead's call.

Life Is a Journey is, of course, one story, and at its base are his late mother's words to "let God be first and foremost in your life, and if you do, God will bless you for His glory."[2] I want to suggest at least three significant storylines embedded in this one story: the immigrant story; the ministry story; and the faith/faithfulness story.

Human migration throughout the world is not a new phenomenon; human beings have been seeking better lives "someplace else" since the beginning of time. Jamaican emigration had begun during the latter 19th century especially to Panama, and in the 1940–1950s to post-war reconstruction in the United Kingdom. It has been estimated that over 1 million Jamaicans emigrated from Jamaica

---

[1] I no longer know the source of this quote but remember Mead's reported comment as she launched the Oral History Project at Columbia University.

[2] Ivy-Ann Peynado.

between the 1970's to 2008, with the United States receiving consistently larger numbers (82%) than the United Kingdom and Canada.[3] Pastor Peynado's migration journey, like so many others, was not a straight-line journey. As he makes clear, his goal destination was the United States, and this line went first to England, then to New York City, then back to England, and finally to the United States. Along the way, there were 1-step back/2-steps back episodes, disappointments, hard decisions, amazing victories, and above all, a growing network of old and new partners for the journey.

Pastor Peynado's migration story was his family's journey as well, and he shares some very precious moments. As a fortunate reader, I was blessed by his retelling of his courtship of his soon-to-be wife Nomey Agatha Reid, and of his joy in being a father. I was also deeply moved as he shared the last moments and poignant last words of his dying young son. Along the way, the family was able to continue their forward movement with the unselfishness of other Jamaican families sharing their homes, their churches, their support, and their prayers. This pattern of diaspora networks providing sustenance, job help, and important contacts has played out time and again in the U. S. (including in my own family), whether original homelands were the Atlantic, Caribbean, or Pacific Islands; Asia; central, eastern, or western Europe; or South America.[4] These diverse global populations have contributed enormously to the U.S., contradicting the 2019 context of growing anti-immigrant sentiment.

The second story is Pastor Peynado's journey and calling to the ministry. His bedrock belief in the power of education and to learning from every situation are consistently displayed. He always kept his eyes on the next educational goal, just as with the goals of migration to the U.S. and of completing the new church. As an exemplary lifelong learner, he strived to be and do his best wherever he was:

---

[3] Glennie, Alex and Chappell, Laura, 6/16/2010, "Jamaica: From Diverse Beginning to Diaspora in the Developed World," In *the Online Journal: Migration Policy Institute,* page 4.

[4] These same patterns and networks can be found in contemporary migration from African countries, but that would require a larger explanation of the historical slavery story that cannot be told here.

British Railway laborer, sole proprietor of his own establishment, or Senior Pastor. Furthermore, he understood that some but not all the skills of a successful sole proprietor were transferable to pastoring a congregation. The new setting required some other skills such as collaboration, communication, and listening. The fact that he discerned and addressed this can be instructive, especially for bi-vocational or 2nd-career ministers, or for those responsible for training them.

Pastor Peynado's determined faith and his trust in God's faithfulness are shown most dramatically as he recounts the inspiring story of building—and then re-building after a fire—the new church. At the most impossible junctures, unexpected help came from equally unexpected sources. He understood well that his own faith was always empowered by God's faithfulness, even after "counting the cost"[5] and always praying. He understood the importance of the network and community who were there at every stage, and he acknowledges and thanks them all. Throughout the challenging (and, I'm sure, some hair-pulling moments) process, his heart, mind, and spirit seem tethered to the long-ago words of his mother. As I consider my own engagement with his book, I realize that his mother's words were not so much that her son would be blessed but rather that the whole miraculous journey would glorify God. I thank you, Pastor Peynado…

—Laura Pires-Hester, PhD
2019

The book you are about to read is one more volume of what I would summarize as the testimony of; a Leader, a legend, and a legacy of an incredible journey'.

In these pages, Michael Peynado shows how the faith principles from the scriptures unfolded in his life from birth that helped him develop and grow as a Christian to stay on the pathway of righteous living which kept him focused regardless of the uncertainties ahead. His life story is confirmation of the Word of God, "Train up a child

---

[5] Luke 14:28 (KJV).

in the way he should go; even when he is old, he will not depart from it (NASB).

I believe Michael Peynado to be one of the most faithful, committed and genuine men of integrity I have met in ministry and public life. I have cherished this man of God as a friend, colleague, mentor and above all a trustworthy believer. His honesty to be transparent as crystal and shares the details of his life's journey; the struggles, challenges, pitfalls, successes and accomplishments is a true testimony of who this Pastor really is and one who I have trusted to model my life after. Yes indeed, this book is a testimony that he practices what he preaches.

Rev. Peynado has masterfully outlines how we should function within the context of Biblical living and gives us pause how we should relate to others within our family, the Body of Christ and public life.

He shows us how the progressive accomplishments and successes has been confirmed by the Holy Spirit through intercession and consultation with his family system and his own ministry leaders. Pastor Peynado is truly a 21st century hero of the faith.

God has given us a visionary, a leader, a legend and a legacy that has and will impact many generations following to pursue their dreams and vision to experience God and fulfill their God-given purposes in life.

I am privileged to be a mentee and recipient of the overflow from the blessed life of The Right Reverend Michael Peynado.

Thank you for calling us back to live out the principles of the Bible.

—Rev. Dr. Harold E. Banarsee
President
Eastern New York General assembly of the Church of God

Rev. Peynado is a godly highly motivated man who has a passion for things that are honest, things that are lovely and things that are of a good report. Michael Peynado from his early childhood was influenced by godly, humble and hardworking parents. Like all good parents who love their children, they wanted the best for Michael in every way.

Michael was born in Jamaica, immigrated to the United Kingdom and then to the United States of America. In his life journey, Michael discovered that there is nothing too hard for God to do. When there seemed to be no way out, God's Word reassured him that Jesus is the way, the truth and the life. All things are possible to those who believe in God, in themselves and see the best in people.

In his autobiography, Michael exhibits that he is a person of faith. From the ordinary to the extraordinary God worked on his behalf during his trials, tribulations and tempests. Hardships and sufferings were not problems to Michael because of his strong faith in God. Almighty God, who is omnipotent worked on his behalf. 1 John 5: 4–5 tells us. "Everyone born of God overcomes the world, this is the victory that has overcome the world, even our faith. Who is it that overcomes the world? Only he who believes that Jesus is the Son of God."

In his life's journey, it was faith in God that gave Michael bountiful blessings to make his hopes and dreams come to fruition. Although he was in the valley of despair, he did not wallow in circumstances, and conditions that he encountered. With optimism, giving thanks to God, he experienced the power of prayer and praise.

—Rev. Dr. Charles C. Collymore
Senior Pastor,
United Community Church of God
June 2019

ACKNOWLEDGMENTS

My heartfelt gratitude goes to my beloved Wife Nomey. She has been an inspiration and an encourager to me in writing this Book, (Life is a Journey). I have denied her countless hours of my time, to write this book. Now that it's completed, she is very appreciative of my accomplishment and look forward to spend quality time with my Granddaughter Abigail and me.

Our granddaughter, Abigail Ayala authored her own book

Abigail who is also an Author, wrote her first book, "The Museum" at the tender age seven. She is now ten and is very proud to choose the covering of this Book.

Thanks to our Daughters Marion and Merna who have read the contents of "Life is a Journey" and sanctioned their approval.

Thanks must go also to Rev. Dr. Harold Banarsee, who has been helpful in critique-ting and made recommendation to enhance, "Life is a Journey."

Thanks to Deaconess Hyacinth McKen, who poured over the contents; "Life is a journey," did editing and made recommendations and gave encouragements.

I am grateful to Dr. Marie Ramsay, Dr. Charles Collymore and Dr. Author W. Davenport, for their insight shared wisdom, encouragement and ideas. My sincere gratitude to Dr. Laura Pires-Hester, who along with my other colleagues have poured over the contents and made recommendations.

Thanks to my Niece Cynthia Thompson, we attended the same elementary school at Bath, St. Thomas, Jamaica West Indies. She has been an inspiration to me in writing this Book. My appreciation also goes to her daughter, my Grand Niece Sherille Rivera for her excitement when I told her of my writings.

My sincere gratitude to all my endorsers and all those who have played a part in me writing, "Life is a Journey." Thanks to the late Dr. Melvin Hester, one of my teachers at CBI, who have helped to shape my thinking in broadening the scope of my writing, thanks also to Dr. Whitfield Blenman, Dean of CBI, a great motivator? I am grateful for Trinity College and Theological Seminary who have inspired me through much deeper learning.

First, I must ascribe all glory, honor, and praise to Jesus Christ my Savior. Without Him, I could not have embarked on this journey. My dear mother, Ivy-Ann Peynado, told me when I was growing up, "Son, let God be first in your life's journey, and if you do, He will work all things to His glory for you." I was young and did not understand; but as I grew older, I realized that her counsel was invaluable. I did not know where this journey would lead me. However, looking back over my early childhood—starting with my early schooling, trade school, migration from Jamaica, West Indies, to England and to the United States of America—I can truly say that this has been a rewarding journey.

I am of the belief in John Donne's words: "No man is an island, entire of itself."[6] So I would be remiss if I did not mention those who assisted me along the way. The following families were the early pioneers who helped to birth the Westbury Divine Church of God, along with my wife and myself, Pastor Michael and Nomey Peynado: Rev. George A. Johnson, Rev. Euton, Sylvia Watson, Adam Dawkins and Hortense Dawkins, Joe Heath Redfern, Henrietta Redfern, Calvin Morris and Viola Morris. *Their sacrificial contributions were immeasurable.* I will never be able to repay them for their faithfulness, their dedication, and their generosity. They will go down in the history of the Westbury Divine Church of God as the bedrock of the church.

Many other ministers, deacon, deaconess, and members came along later to enhance this ministry, bringing us to where we are today. These include the late Rev. Renecca and Rev. Arthur Pinnock; Min. Milton Martin and his wife, Sister Cordelia Martin; Rev. Annette Ridley and Deacon Dudley Ridley; Rev. Dr. Marie Ramsay and Deacon Harlan Ramsay; Rev. Benjamin Chambers and Sister Marjorie Chambers; Rev. Philmon Moulton; Min. Alcita Moulton. Deaconess Hyacinth McKen came on board as secretary and women's connection ministry leader and took those two departments to another level by equipping others to be effective leaders in her department.

These and many others came alongside me on this journey. The appendix provides a fuller listing of church leaders and their respective positions.

I am humbled and forever grateful to God, my wife and family, and all who have joined me on this journey. To God be the glory.

---

[6] John Donne, "Meditation XVII," in *Devotions upon Emergent Occasions* (1624).

INTRODUCTION

Let God be first and foremost in your life.

—Ivy-Ann Peynado

Life is indeed a journey. From birth, I embarked on this journey, not knowing where it would lead. I did not know the pitfalls or successes that lay ahead. However, one thing I did know was there was no retreat, detour, or exit for an alternate route.

While growing up as a child, I learned something very important from my mother: to let God be first and foremost in my life; and if I do, He will bless me for His glory. I have often thought about what she said, and as I write this book, I reflect on Abram/Abraham in the Bible. God had called him, and said, "Get thee out of your country, and from your kindred and from your father's house unto a land that I will show you…I will bless you and bless them that bless you" (Genesis 12:1–2, KJV).

When Abram embarked on his journey, he did so by faith. Because of his faith, he is regarded by many biblical scholars as the "father of faith." He had no idea where he was going or what would befall him, but he took God at His word and moved out by faith, and God kept His promise to him.

In a similar way, when I embarked on this journey, it was all by faith, with Jesus as my guide. I started with limited life experiences. I had no formal education, trade, or hope of emigrating. I had no plans for marriage, having a family, or being the administrator of my own business or a church. Neither did I know that I would be ministering, feeding, and clothing the needy nationally and internationally, or addressing domestic violence or geriatric issues. I am convinced that all of these were already in God's plan when He took charge of my life.

Now, will you come with me on this journey?

1
CHAPTER

My Early Years in Jamaica West Indies

Wherewithal shall a young man cleanse his ways
but by taking heed to the Word of God.

—Psalm 119:9

My name is Michael Peynado. I was born in the parish of Bath, St. Thomas, Jamaica, West Indies, on December 22, 1938, to the late Eugene Peynado and Ivy-Ann Peynado. I was the eighth of nine children. My father was a farmer and ranger, my mother was a home-maker, and together they had nine children: Joel Strachan, Olga Strachan and Amy Strachan were born to my mother's first husband. He went to Cuba in search of work and never returned to Jamaica. My father Eugene Peynado, met and marry my mother Ivy. In that union, they had, Parkey, Stephen, Evelyn, Michael and Sylvia. My father was the sole breadwinner. His meager income was one English pound per week, which was equivalent to two American dollars then. He had to depend on crops from his farm to feed our family; and of course, the crops were heavily dependent upon weather conditions. It was not easy for my parents to sustain a family of nine children and provide us a good education on such a meager income.

My Schooling

I attended Bath Elementary School in my district at the age of seven. I can remember the excitement I had when I went to school with two brothers and three sisters that first Monday morning. However, when I walked into my classroom, I saw one of the teachers using a strap as corporal punishment on one of the little children (mercilessly). As I recall, that child was in my class. At that moment, I froze. No longer was I excited to be in school or to go back to school. I was afraid that if I made mistakes, the same punishment would be meted out to me with a belt or cane.

Some of the teachers didn't take time with children they assumed to be slow learners, and they used the cane or strap as punishment to force them to learn. I presumed I was among the slow learners when one of the teachers hit me with a ruler on my head and called me "duffer." From that moment on, I was no longer interested in school and started cutting classes.

Sometime later, I looked up the word "duffer" and discovered that it referred to an incompetent person. I have since learned of course that no child is incompetent unless there is some chemical imbalance in the brain. Given the appropriate teacher with the right approach, every child can learn.

Grade 1 through the fourth grade were very turbulent times for me. After the fourth grade, I was promoted to the fifth grade, not because I was smart but because of my age. The same thing happened in my other grades.

In fifth grade, I had a teacher whose name was Ms. Lawrence. I will never forget the first day I spent in her class. She made me feel welcomed and gave me the assurance that I could learn. She told me not to stay away from school because I would soon be leaving and facing the real world, and an education is very important. Her encouragement and warning were so correct. Still, I skipped school for up to three weeks at a time, against the will of my parents and teachers, using my school lunch money or bag lunch to pay off my sisters not to tell my parents.

When I was about fifteen years old, I decided that it was just too late for me to catch up with the foundational subjects that I had missed. I could not read a book and make sense of it. Neither could I comprehend the other subjects beyond the basic ones, of which I had no concept at all. I was beginning to learn how important it was for Ms. Lawrence's cautioning statement back in the fifth grade.

Then I was placed in the sixth grade, again because of my age. In that grade, I had a hostile teacher who believed in punishing children with the cane. I became fearful and started skipping school once more. One day, when I had skipped school, I got a message from my teacher stating that my time was expired. At first, I was excited, and it didn't matter to me; but after a few weeks, I realized how foolish I was. I was now facing the real world and did not have a formal education to prepare me for the future. Ms. Lawrence's cautionary words came back to haunt me, but it was too late. Elementary school was over, and I was facing the real world.

Neglecting the counsel of my parents and teachers and willfully not staying in school were some of my biggest mistakes. Wasted time can never be retrieved, and regret is the thief of time. The only option I had was trade school. My parents did not have the money for me to take private lessons.

After elementary school, which all my siblings completed, we were given the opportunity to learn a trade. Two of my brothers learned shoemaking, one masonry, and I learned tailoring. My sisters were all involved with some form of dressmaking. Looking back, I can say we were very fortunate that our parents were wise enough to have us learn a trade. Even though they themselves had minimal formal education, they knew it was very important for us to have an education and/or an occupation.

Later in life, I realized that what they did for us was something they were not privileged to have. To our parents, it was very important for us to grow up and have a family and not experience the same poverty that they did. My mother had encouraged me to let God be first in my life. She also encouraged me to learn a trade that would help me on life's journey.

In 1957, my parents placed me into a tailoring establishment at Bath, St. Thomas, to learn tailoring with Dinston Jullal. I stayed with that establishment, where I learned to surge pants and make buttonholes by hand. After approximately two months with that establishment, my parents sent me to Kingston, the capital of Jamaica, to further develop my tailoring skills with a relative, Bishop Henry Solomon Ellis, an accomplished tailor, he taught me more skills but also the art of the tailoring trade, which really helped prepare me for my life's journey.

While I was with Bishop Ellis and my late cousin Anita Ellis, they invited me to the Church of the First Born in Kingston. A young man, Brother Ward, preached on the scripture, "Wherewithal shall a young man cleanse his ways? By taking heed there-to according to thy word" (Psalm 119:9, KJV). From that moment on, I was convinced of the reality of the saving grace of our Lord Jesus Christ, and I made a commitment to follow Him for the rest of my life. This led me to taking many biblical instruction classes; and later in 1957, I was baptized by the late Pastor F. S. Bent at Church of the First Born in Jonestown, Kingston, Jamaica. I was very happy in my newfound life and continued going to Sunday school and church. I was learning more about Christ and the Bible and the winning of souls for His kingdom.

My passion for Him took me to the streets of Kingston to proclaim the good news of salvation. It was very rewarding to see unsaved people who came forward to receive Christ as their personal Savior, and this gripped my heart. All of this made for a very productive three years spent with Bishop Ellis, being coached in the Christian faith while also learning the craft of tailoring.

Emigration to England and Marriage

I was very fashion conscious and had a passion to learn more about the fashion and design industry. As God's plan would have it, my brother Stephen invited me to England in 1960. I accepted the invitation and went to the British Embassy in Kingston to apply for a British passport. After many months of waiting, I received a call from the embassy that the passport was granted. In September 1960, I left for England on a ship.

I was told that the ship would take seventeen days to reach England. After three days on board, my burning desire to worship God and preach the Gospel propelled me to ask the captain for permission to have religious services on board. Without hesitation, he showed me a place on the second deck for the service.

When I approached the captain with my request, I did not know if it would be granted; neither did I think it was an unusual request. I thought there could only be two answers, yes or no; thank God, yes prevailed. I went around and invited many people to the service; some were believers, and some were nonbelievers. However, for the rest of the journey, the gospel of Christ was preached, and souls were saved and gave their testimonies of their newfound life in Christ.

When I arrived in England, it was a cold and cloudy September day. I saw smoke billowing from all the buildings, so I thought that they were all factories. However, I soon realized that they were homes, and I would be living in one of them. In those days, there was no central heating. Therefore, for homes to be heated, coals were used in the furnace, and from the furnace, the smoke went up the chimney, which created the view that made me think the houses were factories. Nonetheless, I felt blessed to have arrived in England.

My primary goal was to further develop my tailoring skills and to be a fashion designer. My plan was to return then to my home island, establish myself, and help develop my homeland. Unfortunately, I could not get into a designing school in England. The schools' standards were much too advanced for me. I was disappointed but not dismayed because I knew that on this journey, my steps were ordered by the Lord.

At this juncture, I desperately needed a job. For about three months, I walked every day of the week, except Sundays, seeking a job. Having one pair of shoes on my feet and no replacement, my shoes began to wear thin, with holes in the bottom. However, no one told me that the journey would be easy or of the pitfalls that I would encounter.

Finally, I got a job with the British Railway as a laborer. I was handed a pair of overalls, a shovel, a wheelbarrow, and a broom by the foreman. I had to work in a locomotive yard, sweeping up coals that fell from steam engines. Back in Jamaica, that would have been very humiliating for me. However, having experienced what it was like not to have a job and almost barefooted in a cold country, I was very happy to get one. It did not matter what kind of job, as long as I was working for an honest living.

Nevertheless, my ambition kept propelling me forward, reminding me that this was not what I came to England to do. After a short period on the job, I was offered the opportunity to go to school and learn to be a signalman with the same company; that did not work out. However, I got a job in one of their offices as a clerk, and I worked in that position until I applied to work on the train as a passenger guard.

While working for the British Railway, I enrolled in the Ebenezer Bible Institute in Birmingham to enhance my knowledge in biblical studies in preparation for whatever ministry the Lord had in store for me. At the Bible institute, my teacher Pastor Radcliff Joseph was a great encourager, motivator, and inspiration. He helped to mold and shape me for ministry. Although I did not know that one day I would be a pastor, he saw something in me and brought the best out of me. While still attending Bible school, I also set my eyes on someone I recognized as my soul mate, who was in nursing school at the time.

It was while I was attending United Pentecostal Assembly in Birmingham, UK, where my brother Joel Strachan was the pastor, that I met my wife-to-be, Nomey Agatha Reid, later Nomey Agatha Peynado. She too had emigrated from Jamaica, West Indies, to study nursing in England. I had observed her over a period of time, in the church and outside the church, and realized that she was of outstanding character. She was a devoted, dedicated, and ambitious young Christian lady.

I approached her and asked if she would marry me. She assured me that she would if I could wait until her nursing studies were completed. I waited patiently for her. In 1966, after she completed her studies, we were married at West Bromwich Methodist Church in Birmingham, England.

Our first home as a married couple was at her uncle's home at 43 Hallam Street, West Bromwich, Birmingham, and our first child, Marion, was born in 1967 at Hallam Hospital in Birmingham. This was a very happy time in our lives, but we needed more room with our growing family. We moved into a bigger space at 14 St. Peters Road, Lozells, Birmingham, which was the home of our friends the Donaldsons. It was then that I had the opportunity to go on a vacation to the USA.

American Interval, 1969

I was always hoping for an opportunity to go to the United States of America. I had heard it was a land of beauty and great possibilities. In 1969, my sister Olga, who was living in the USA, was planning to get married and invited me to her wedding. I went to the US Embassy in London and applied for a visa; and within a few months, I received it.

It was very disheartening for me to leave my wife alone with our newborn child. Nevertheless, we had decided that it was the right thing to do in order to explore new possibilities for our family. In March of that year, I came on a vacation to America, and upon arrival in New York, I experienced one of the worst snowstorms I had ever experienced—reportedly, the worst New York had ever had.

Other than that first winter experience, I soon fell in love with New York because of its cultural diversity; and after a few weeks, I started inquiring about how to acquire a visa to immigrate to the US with my family. Because of the demands for nurses here in the US, my wife's now being a registered nurse in England was our best opportunity for obtaining a permanent visa. So I went to Queens General Hospital in Queens, New York and inquired about her possible sponsorship. They jumped at the opportunity to sponsor her for employment and gave me all the necessary paperwork to start the process.

Upon my return to the UK six months later, I filed the necessary papers with the American Embassy in London. While waiting for our exit papers, we moved from 14 St. Peters Road in Lozells, Birmingham, to our new apartment at 9 Murdock Point in Erdington, Birmingham, where our son Joseph, who is now deceased, was born in 1970.

As a young couple with young children, we were experiencing a very tight schedule; however, this was all a part of our journey. My wife and I were both working full-time jobs, and I was going to school in the evenings while also working different shifts. Only through teamwork could we balance rearing our two children and maintaining our household at the same time.

I loved being a father. It gave me so much joy to spend time with our children. I became adept at combing out Marion's hair and dressing her and Joseph. I loved taking them out in the pram for our regular stroll in the botanical garden where we enjoyed looking at the beautiful flowers, watching fish swim in the ponds, and taking beautiful pictures. The beautiful smiles on their faces and their wonderful laughter made it all worthwhile.

Living in England was very enlightening, and I was exposed to a wide range of cultures and interactions with people from different parts of the world. However, remembering that my initial goal was to get an education, make a lot of money, and go back to my native land Jamaica to help in its development, I did not see the opportunity in England to achieve this goal. Although being in England brought me some success, and I gained much experience there, my eyes were nevertheless still on the United States of America. Spending six months there had whetted my desire for the success I know we could attain in the US. I could see that there was no limitation to one's achievements, so securing a visa to immigrate to the States would be ideal for my family and me.

Visa to America

The wait for a permanent visa to America seemed to be never-ending. We made numerous visits from Birmingham to the embassy in London for our updated status. In 1972, two and a half years later, we got the long-awaited call from the embassy, stating the visa was granted. That was one of the happiest moments for me.

However, such a drastic transition to leave the known for the unknown was not so easy for my wife. She was well established in her career and had been promoted to nursing supervisor (called a "sister" at the hospital). She was very concerned about such a radical move. I assured her that she would not be disappointed; America was a beautiful place, and she would love living there. On May 6, 1972, my family and I immigrated to the USA. We stayed in the Bronx, New York, with the Dawkins family, thus beginning a new chapter in our lives.

Upon arrival, we learned that there was a freeze at the hospital that had sponsored my wife, so both of us were having difficulties finding employment. With two children to care for, rent to pay, and other expenses, we had to make a very painful decision for Nomey to take the children to live with her parents in Jamaica. That would give us the opportunity we needed to vigorously seek employment.

While my wife was away, I got my first tailoring job working with a dry-cleaning agency. My first paycheck was twenty dollars per day, which left much to be desired and not enough to cover our expenses. Upon my wife's return from Jamaica, we were still having difficulties getting employment in the city. We decided to move to Long Island where the possibility of getting employment was much better.

Our two good friends Euton and Sylvia Watson had invited us to come and live with them in Westbury, Long Island; and within a few weeks, both of us had jobs. Mine was in a department store, selling shoes. Of course, I had never sold shoes before, but I was happy and willing to learn. The manager taught me well; and within a few months, I became one of the top salespersons. My wife, a registered nurse from England, was hired as a nursing assistant while she pursued the licensing required for hiring as a registered nurse in the United States.

Now that we were both employed, we were very eager to purchase a home so that our children could rejoin us. With that in mind, I got another job as a uniform salesman and also become an entrepreneur selling Knapp shoes. With an optimistic approach, my wife and I saved enough cash by 1973 to make a down payment on our first home at 183 Bedford Avenue, Garden City Park, New York. The price of the house was $33,500, and the monthly mortgage payment was $360.

Our daughter, Maron
Peynado-Ayala

Our daughter, Merna Pettit

Grandson Marcus McFarlane

Our great granddaughters
Aniyah and Ariyanna McFarlane

Grandson Joshua Pettit

Grandson
Matthew Pettit

Grandson Joseph Pettit

God continued putting the pieces together in our lives. My wife completed her training, got her degree, and was employed as a registered nurse. We wrote to the children's grandmother in Jamaica and asked her to bring our children to us. Before we were married, I had a precious daughter Merna who was born in England prior to our marriage. We were very excited when she too came and joined us in the USA. It was one of our happiest moments to have our three children with us. Our children, whom we loved and missed so much, had joined us again. Life was complete. We were together again, so I decided to launch out into new possibilities.

Experiences in Our New Homeland

In 1973, I was fortunate to have two jobs, one as a shoe salesman in a department store, and the other a postal uniform salesman. On the weekends, I was an entrepreneur selling Knapp shoes. In that same year, I started night school to study for my GED. I knew that this would not be easy. Nonetheless, I purposed in my heart that this would be one of my accomplishments; and in 1974, I graduated with my diploma. That was an outstanding achievement for me, and it began my quest to further my education in my new homeland.

Having received my diploma, I focused on getting a college education. I enrolled in Nassau Community College, majoring in psychology and English. I also enrolled in Christian Bible Institute in Freeport, Long Island, to advance my biblical knowledge. Upon completion of the theological course, I received a certificate in Christian education.

In 1974, the same year that I was called by God to the ministry, I was ordained as a minister by the late Bishop Oliver Corbin and the late Rev. Crafton Thompson. As a willing volunteer, I served under the leadership of Rev. Crafton Thompson, engaged in teaching, preaching, and performing other related duties as directed by the Holy Spirit.

While serving in these roles, I still held three jobs—one a uniform salesperson, another a shoes salesperson, and the third one was selling Knapp shoes as my own business—while taking care of my family. At this time, an opportunity opened to purchase a tailoring establishment at 144 Post Avenue in Westbury, New York. I did not have the money to purchase the establishment. Nevertheless, acting on faith, I went to a bank in my community and applied for a loan. I was met with obstacles: my wife and I did not have enough money in our bank account as collateral, and our combined jobs did not generate enough money to meet the monthly payment.

We had just purchased our new home, and a business would be ideal to generate needed income. I did not fall into discouragement because I could see the possibilities. I also had Jesus on my side, who is truly my "collateral." I prayed and asked Him for favor. He heard my persistent prayers, and I was able to negotiate and secure a loan for four thousand dollars, the amount needed to purchase the establishment. I renovated the store and converted it into a retail store. I sold women and men's apparels and utilized a section for tailoring and alterations.

This was certainly an exciting time for me, managing my own business for the first time. I gave credit first to Almighty God for being in the United States of America, where doors were opened for me, an immigrant with no cash flow, to start a business in a predominantly Caucasian community. I was well accepted in the community because of the quality of my merchandise, my knowledge, and my workmanship.

Being my own boss at thirty-seven was a great achievement. I had hoped that by the age of fifty, I would become a millionaire, my children would be out of college, and I would retire to Jamaica and enjoy the good life. However, I was bothered by a scripture: "for what is a man profited, if he shall gain the whole world, and lose his own soul? Or what shall a man give in exchange for his soul?" (Matthew 16:26, TCRB). From that moment on, my ministry became real, and my passion to serve Christ grew deeper. His calling on my life was evident in my spirit.

2
CHAPTER

THE COMMENCEMENT OF MY MINISTRY

For which of you, intending to build a tower, sitteth not down first, and counteth the cost, whether he have sufficient to finish it?

—Luke 14:28 (KJV)

In 1975, my passionate call to the pastorate was solidified when Pastor George A. Johnson, who knew me from England, came to the USA and met with me. He knew that I had attended Ebenezer Bible Institute in Birmingham, England, and he encouraged me and my wife, Rev. Euton and Sister Sylvia Watson, Deacon Adam and Deaconess Hortense Dawkins, and Franklin Golding to start a Christian ministry in our home. We decided to do this with prayer meetings held at the Dawkins home, youth meetings at the Watson home, and Sunday worship services at the Peynado home.

Pastor Johnson's encouragement confirmed the call of God upon my life. We decided to have a meeting at the Dawkins home at 226 Hopper Street in Westbury, New York, to appoint leaders for the ministry that was about to commence. Attending this important meeting were Rev. Johnson, Deacon Adam and Deaconess Hortense Dawkins, Rev. Euton and Sister Sylvia Watson and Rev. Michael and Sister Nomey Peynado. I was appointed by the group to be the pastor,

Reverend Watson to be the assistant pastor, Deacon Dawkins as treasurer, Sister Watson as secretary, and Sister Peynado as Sunday school superintendent and head of Christian education. We all accepted our different roles. I was still the sole proprietor of my own business.

I did not know exactly where the Lord was leading or how I could handle the administrative demands of my business along with my new assignment for God. However, when I met with Pastor Johnson, a seasoned pastor, he assured me that I was indeed able to do what God wanted me to do. From that moment on, I became confident in my spirit that God had called me, and I made a full commitment to pursue a career in ministry.

After conferring with the three families, we diligently sought the Lord through prayer and fasting for a dwelling place to house the church. Our first attempt was disappointing, but we did not give up. In 1978, I was shown a 1.9-acre land with overgrown shrubberies, trees, and a dilapidated building. This plot of land was on the southwestern side of Brush Hollow Road in the Village of Westbury. We looked over the land; and with the consensus of all members, we decided to purchase it, not knowing where the finances would come from.

Finances to Purchase the Land

In our pursuit of the necessary resources, we first approached our local church assembly (ENYGA) and our national headquarters (COGM) in Anderson, Indiana, for financial support. The attempts were discouraging. Again and again, we heard reasons why it was impossible to purchase the land: number 1, we were few in numbers; number 2, we had no money; and number 3, they had seen others go this way before, and it did not work out.

However, I knew that God had given us this piece of land. I remembered Joshua, who had sent men to spy out the land of Canaan and similarly saw many discouraging things. First, there was the Jordan River, and then there were formidable giants in the land. Still, after they had spied out the land, they reported to Joshua: "Truly the LORD hath delivered unto us all the land: for even all the inhabitants of the country faint because of us" (Joshua 2:24, TCRB).

Joshua could have become fainthearted, but his God-given courage propelled him forward to possess the land. So too with us; we could have been discouraged being a new church planting and having no money for the purchase. Nonetheless, we continued to pray to the Lord Jesus Christ. Three families—namely Deacon Adam and Hortense Dawkins, Rev. Michael and Nomey Peynado, and Rev. Euton and Sylvia Watson— pledged six thousand dollars per family toward the down payment of twenty-five thousand dollars. Considering our wages in those days, this was a major sacrifice. I then led the three families in a fund-raising campaign; and within one year, we raised thirty thousand dollars, which is over and above the necessary funds for the down payment.

Founding Members Rev. Euton
and Sylvia Watson

Having purchased the property, I "counted the cost" of the monumental tasks of clearing the land and renovating the dilapidated building. This seemed insurmountable, knowing that the necessary funds were not available. However, I was reminded about Psalm 78:19: "Can God furnish a table in the wilderness?" The children of Israel were in the wilderness and became discouraged because they could not see a way out, so they questioned that God would deliver them. Yet God did provide food when they were hungry, meat when needed, and water when they were thirsty. So, resoundingly, yes, He can provide a "table in the wilderness." God has always been a great provider.

We continued to pray earnestly to Him for help to clear the land and renovate the dilapidated building. Our prayers were answered. God chose the late Brother Joe Heath Redfern to send us men, women, tractors, trucks, and bulldozers to clear the land, all for free. Brother Raymond Terry and his men voluntarily worked to renovate the dilapidated building and convert it into a church. It took us approximately one year and seven months to complete.

THE WESTBURY TIMES – JULY 16, 1998

911 BRUSH HOLLOW ROAD as it appeared in 1980, shortly before the Westbury Divi Congregational Church of God took over the property and completely refurbished it.

Late into the Thursday night before Good Friday in 1980, we were putting on finishing touches so that the building would be ready for our Good Friday and Easter Sunday services. There was a fireplace in the building, and the young men were stoking it with wood to keep us warm. We were excited about what Jesus had made possible and looking forward to worshipping on that Good Friday and Easter Sunday. However, this journey was not without pitfalls.

Early on Good Friday morning, I received a call from the village fire marshal, who informed me that the church was on fire. It was devastating news. However, on this journey, we never know what lies ahead. One thing I did know: God was still in charge. It was a blessing that the building was not completely destroyed. The late Brother Wilbert Morgan from another church, who had been working on our building pro bono, told me that he would donate the Sheetrock needed to repair the damage. What a blessing that was! We were able to renovate the building and worship within a few weeks.

I realized that as a young minister, my faith was being tested. Not very long after that, my wife drove our car to the shopping mall, and it was stolen. Then our only son, Joseph, was stricken with lymphatic leukemia at the tender age of seven and a half. Looking back, I think of the song, "Nobody told me the road would be easy, but I don't believe He brought me this far to leave me."[1] I knew that the enemy was trying to derail the ministry that God had called me to do. The more he attacked, the more the Lord strengthened me for the journey. Before my son became sick, he gave his heart to the Lord; and while he was in the hospital, he requested water baptism.

While he was in remission, we brought him home, and we administered water baptism unto him. He had medical treatments for the next three years in and out of remission. During those three years, the family created some of our fondest memories of him. We went fishing, swimming, soccer, and jogging, among other things. At ten and a half years old in 1979, he spent his last Christmas with us at home. The day after Christmas, I was taking him back to the

---

[1] Rev. James Cleveland/Curtis Burrell, "I Don't Feel No Ways Tired."

hospital for treatment, and I recall his saying, "I won't be coming back home."

I said, "Son, how do you know that?"

He began to cry. As a father, those words pierced my heart, but I could not show him my emotion because he needed my strength. He was right. He passed away at Long Island Jewish Hospital in January 1980. His mother and I were by his bedside, watching him fade into eternity. His parting words were, "Goodbye, life. It was nice knowing you. Mom and Dad had lots of kisses in the cup for me."

In loving memory of our son Joseph Peynado

Those words broke our hearts. Our one and only son was about to leave us permanently. We knew that he was very excited and looking forward to being a part of our newly renovated church. Now he would never get to do so.

Only those who have experienced it can know the pain of losing a child so dear and close to one's heart. At the same time, I know that my God never makes a mistake. He gives life, and He takes it. It was not for me to question Him or ask why because whatever He does is done well.

For those who are going through or have gone through this same situation, I encourage you to be strong in the Lord and in the power of His might. He has a plan and a purpose for your life. Sometimes, the unthinkable happens for Him to carry out His plan. On life's journey, time will never erase one's memory, but time will soothe the pain and bring comfort through Jesus Christ our Redeemer and King.

New Church Location

March on Brush Hollow Road to newly renovated edifice

In 1980, we relocated the Westbury Divine Church of God to its new location at 911 Brush Hollow Road, Westbury, New York. The town blocked off two major highways for us so that we could celebrate the opening with a march from Prospect Avenue and Brush Hollow Road, with the Nassau County Police Department leading; the Boy Scouts in the middle, playing music and beating their drums; and the fire department behind. It was an outdoor celebration, and we had one of the largest tents, which could accommodate approximately one thousand people. Mayor Ernie Strada and other dignitaries from the Village of Westbury attended. The late Dr. Lavern Aaron was the speaker; he commented that it was the largest tent he had ever seen. We give all the honor, glory, and praise to God for what He had done. It was certainly a momentous occasion that will never be forgotten, as recorded in the annals of these pages.

Service under the tent 1980 to celebrate the renovated edifice

I was passionate about using my business administrative skills to enhance God's kingdom. I began reading books and attending seminars and courses related to pastoring. I did not have any practical administrative skills in the church setting; however, God had equipped me through my exposure to learning. I recognized that I could utilize some of my business experience in my pastoral ministry but thought I also had to modify some of my administration skills. After all, I realized that I was now in the "people" business, mending hearts through the Word of God rather than mending their clothing. Pastoral demands were more pressing. I had to visit the sick at home, in hospitals, and nursing homes, and feed and clothe the needy. I also performed weddings, baby dedications, funerals, and other related duties.

I also recognized that administering a democratically run church—where every vote matters—was quite different from a sole proprietorship. My administrative experience from my business had to be modified to accommodate the church setting. One of my early mistakes was not sharing enough information with my board, which did not make for the most productive or positive board meetings.

At the beginning of my ministry, I also did not seek out a minister whom I could rely on for administrative coaching. I was leaning on what I saw in other churches and how other pastors carried out their duties, not realizing that every church setting is different. During these early years, I soon recognized that I was becoming too much of a hands-on leader involved in every aspect of church life. Not only did this leave no room for others to learn and grow, it was becoming extremely demanding for me. It took away from my family time and diminished my effectiveness. I was on the road to burnout.

I resolved to change my leadership style and started training and equipping others to do the job. This gave people a feeling of inclusion and self-worth and motivated others to participate in ministry. At the same time, I also acquired new strengths and gained experience in other areas. I am emotionally attached to being an administrative pastor. I feel that my God-given experience is that of helping people, to develop the ministry they are assigned to by God

A New Fund Campaign

The 1,500-square-feet building on the 1.9-acre land at 911 Brush Hollow Road could no longer accommodate all the activities needed to serve our community, so I led the church on a new fund-raising campaign to satisfy our thirty-year mortgage. Thanks be to God, our brothers and sisters, friends and families all rose to the occasion and made great sacrifices. Our efforts were successful, and we paid off our mortgage in seven years. With that done, we continued the campaign to build a new edifice.

The hand of God was in everything that we did. The state decided to widen the road, and they requested nine feet of our property. They paid us $36,500, a little more than half of what we paid for the 1.9-acre land. A portion of our property was also covered with overgrown bamboos that had to be removed. One day, a gentleman came on the property and asked for some of the bamboos. I told him he could have as much as he needed. When he asked the cost, I told him I had no Idea, but a donation would certainly be appreciated. The following day, he returned and handed me a check made out to the church for four thousand dollars. I was overwhelmed, knowing that within a short period, between the widening of the road and the donation for the bamboos, we had collected $40,500. In essence, the property cost us $24,500. This could be none other than the mighty hand of God paving the way for us to build our new church.

Bamboo on the property brought us financial gain

We purchased this prime property for sixty-five thousand dollars. It is in the Village of Westbury between major shopping centers, two major railroad stations, an expressway, three parkways, a turnpike, and two major parks. I could never think of a better location for our church. An emergency number, 911 is a soul-saving station for those who are desperate, downtrodden, and in despair. No wonder God gave us this piece of land to build the new church.

On life's journey, we must always expect the unexpected, especially challenges. But every challenge may provide strength for the journey, and every setback may be a setup for great things. For several years, we had an out-of-town architect draw plans for the new church and presented them to the Village of Westbury. After many meetings and several modified plans and engineering studies requested by the village officials, we finally realized that the village board did not like to work with an out-of-town architect. Compounded with that, they did not like the idea of another church to be built in the village. This information was leaked from their board meeting. Therefore, no matter how many times we presented our plans according to their specifications, our drawings would never be approved. Hence, we had to discontinue that architect's service.

We engaged three different architects and settled with one who was acceptable to the Village of Westbury. During this time, we also engaged four different lawyers, one or more were very unethical. We filed a complaint to the bar association against one lawyer to recoup our retainer's fee. We had given him a five-thousand-dollar fee to represent us at the various meetings. He attended a few times and then stopped communicating with us, so we had no other recourse. The bar association hearing found him guilty of inappropriate attorney-client practice, and he was ordered to return the justifiable funds to us.

Despite these setbacks, the church persevered in praying and fasting over those many years. I never gave up hope because I knew that God had called me to build the church. One night, I went to sleep and had a dream and heard a strong message: "The king's heart is in the hand of the Lord as the rivers of water; He turns it whithersoever He wills" (Proverbs 21:1, TCRB). This message told me that although we have been waiting for ten years, our time is simply not God's timing. If God can turn the heart of a king, then He can most assuredly turn the heart of the village board in our favor. He can accomplish what He had started, and I do not say, "What He had started," lightly.

Many years before I thought about building, the Lord appeared to me in a vision and gave me a blueprint for building the church. I woke up and immediately thought of Habakkuk 2:2: "write the vision and make it plain." I told my wife about the vision and wrote it down on a piece of paper. For many years, I have walked around with that piece of paper in my wallet with great optimism. I knew that God had started this because He gave me the vision. The village board could delay us but could not deny us from building. Galatians 6:9 reminds us not to be "weary in well doing, for in due season we shall reap if we faint not" (TCRB). Thank God we did not faint, but we held on to God's promise. We know that His promise never fails. If we hold on to that promise, He will bring it to pass.

Go-Ahead from the Village Board

I can remember that sad and tragic morning of September 11, 2001 when two airplanes flew into the World Trade Center in New York City. Two of our most majestic buildings were destroyed, and approximately three thousand people were killed. Thousands more were wounded, hospitalized, or otherwise affected.

The enormity of the crisis was overwhelming for our state and country. Mayor Rudolph Giuliani mobilized the city's clergy to provide godly counseling and comfort to the wounded and to grieving families and friends. The liaison assigned to us told us that other secular counselors and organizations were there as well, but they could not meet the immense spiritual and emotional needs of the people. Therefore, they were looking for clergy members who could be further trained in critical crisis management to meet the monumental needs of the people.

Why am I mentioning 9/11? Several people in our community had passed away from the disaster, and among the dead were family members of the village board. We mourned, wept, and prayed for God's covering over our own city, other cities, and our country.

After that tragic day, at our next meeting, the village board gave us the long-awaited requirements necessary for the permit to be granted. As I have mentioned, life is a journey, and no one knows the turn of events that will manifest itself on this journey. One thing is certain: the vision given by God will materialize in His time.

We had attended many, many meetings and spent hundreds of thousands of dollars in legal fees, waiting for the permit to be granted. Those funds would have helped in our construction. I had approached many banks for a construction loan, even banks that the church was doing business with. They all came to the same conclusion; namely, "they don't see the church's ability to pay back the loan." We were making these requests during our country's worst economic crisis in a century and at a time when poverty on Long Island had increased to unprecedented levels.[2] Building a larger edifice with all the amenities to meet the basic needs of the less fortunate would be ideal.

Still, we ascribed all glory and honor to the true and living God because we knew that He must have other plans. We knew that the permit would not have been granted without Him. We serve an awesome God; and even during discouragement, He was the wind beneath our wings, carrying us through the tempestuous storms of adversity. Our journey was not without struggles. However, when God calls you to do a job, never give up; He will see you through to the end.

It took ten years for us to receive the permit from the village. During that time, we continued raising funds and saving those funds in two different banks. In the same month, we received the permit, the Securities and Exchange Commission closed Church Extension of the Church of God, which held the bulk of our funds. Management was ordered to pay off all noteholders in increments of five percent over a five-year period. We had close to one million dollars in that

---

[2] News articles will follow

bank for our immediate use, so that arrangement would not have been beneficial.

Furthermore, we had to start building before the permit expired, and our drawings called for a multi-million-dollar church building. The only other savings we had was $350,000 in another bank. Church members became discouraged and began murmuring and complaining. They had worked very hard to raise and save funds and waited so long for the permit, only to be met with such great disappointment. I was overwhelmed with bewilderment, and I asked myself, "How could such a thing happen to supposedly one of the safest places where we bank the churches' money in a church of God bank?"

However, deep in my spirit, I never heard retreat. Therefore, I encouraged myself and the members through the Word of God and through prayer and fasting, assuring them that the church will be built. I did not know where we would get the funds, but I knew that God had a plan, and that the vision would never die.

In my own prayers and devotions with my wife and other founding members, I reflected on Moses and the struggles he had when he was leading the children of Israel out of Egypt to the Promised Land. They too had murmured and complained when things were not going the way they thought it should, even to the point of wishing to return to Egypt! When they came to the Red Sea, it looked impassable. The Jordan River also looked impassable. But God. Right in front of their eyes, God divided the Red Sea. He divided the Jordan River and made a path for them, except Moses himself, to cross over into the Promised Land.

Sometimes, God will take us through the wilderness of doubt and despair to show us that He is God, and that He will do what He has promised. The Israelites had forgotten that God gave them light to see at night; clouds for direction in the day; and food, meat, and water for sustenance on their journey. So if God can furnish a "table in the wilderness," which He did, is there anything impossible for Him to do for the Westbury Divine Church of God?

Having understood God's wondrous working power, I decided to draw a page from the children of Israel: not to murmur or complain but to call upon the true and living God in prayer. So I asked the church to join me in a season of fasting and prayer. I know that God answers prayer, and He had not told me to retreat despite the financial difficulties. How it would happen, I didn't know, but I just watched miracle after miracle unfurl.

One of our biggest miracles happened when I was invited by Sister Rose Terry to pray for her husband, who was gravely ill in the hospital with a heart rate of sixteen. When I went to see him, I saw a six-foot-three-inch, 250-pound man lying on his back in a hospital bed, weeping like a baby. He had backslidden from his church many years ago. He said, "Pastor, I don't know if God will forgive me for the things that I have done. But if He does, and if He raises me up out of this hospital bed, whatsoever He wants me to do, I will do."

He was not a member of our church, but he knew me well and was very receptive to my visit. I prayed with him and assured him that God is a forgiving God; and if he is sincere with his request, God will answer his prayer. He further said that the doctor had told him that he did not know what was keeping him alive, but whatever it was, he should continue. He stayed in the hospital for a few weeks before leaving with the same heart rate of sixteen.

Brother Terry was a retired construction manager, and God raised him up and gave him a new lease on life. He attended our church and became a member and one of our construction managers. He was, therefore, able to attend many village board meetings where he could discuss technical details of our building project. His prayer was like that of Hezekiah, who turned his face to the wall and prayed to God, reminding Him of his faithfulness:

I beseech thee, O Lord, remember now how I have walked before thee in truth and with a perfect heart, and have done that which is good in thy sight. And Hezekiah wept. The Lord told Isaiah to tell Hezekiah, "I will add unto thy days fifteen years; and I will deliver thee and this city out of the hand of the king of Assyria; and I will defend this city for my own sake, and for my servant David's sake" (2 Kings 20:3,6:TCRB).

Ground Breaking Service

More will be said about Brother Terry and his parting words after the construction was completed. Suffice it to say now that through his effort, we were blessed to break ground on May 9, 2005. After groundbreaking, it took us another one year for the construction managers Bro. Raymond Terry and Neil Lenstrum to be organized; hence, commence working.

While waiting for the construction to begin, we continued our fund-raising campaign. I can remember our accountant saying to me, "Reverend Peynado, I cannot see you building a multi-million-dollar church with the small amount of funds the church has."

I responded that we work by faith and not by sight.

He said he works with numbers, and the numbers that we are showing does not add up. He insisted, "It is impossible to start a project of this magnitude with the funds that we have."

Nevertheless, we went ahead and started construction with the funds we had on hand. When he came by later and saw the mighty handiwork of God in the construction of the building, he said "I will never doubt you again."

Construction vehicle loading

Erection of walls

I must interject here and say again, when God calls you to do a job, don't fall for discouragement. The accountant did not realize that it was not my doing but all about Jesus's doing.

Prayers and Partners during Construction

Sis. Isolene Simmonds the first person at
the commencement of construction

There are so many persons who must be thanked for the parts they played during the construction period. Mother Isolene Simmonds, one of our prayer warriors and encouragers, was one of the first on the scene when construction started. I thank God for Neil Lenstrum and the late Brother Raymond Terry, our construction managers. I also give thanks to Master Electrician Norman Simmonds, the late Brother Carl Terry, Deacon Harlan Ramsay and his son, Rashaad Ramsay and Brother Trevor Burnett, these electricians worked relentlessly in donating their time. I am truly grateful for Rev. Euton Watson, Deacon Richard Laguerre, and the late Sister Smith Woodhouse, who were on the jobsite almost every day to pray with us and help in many other ways.

Right to Left: Construction manager Bro. Raymond
Terry, Rashaad Ramsey, Zeke Marage excavation, Rupert
Aaron masonry, Deacon Harlan Ramsey electrician

Pastor Carlos Andrade and some of his men
who helped with the construction

I give God thanks also for our Hispanic brother, Brother Robert
Hernandez, who came one day and asked if we needed help. I told
him yes; and the next day, he brought his pastor, Pastor Carlos
Andrade, and ten men from his congregation.

Brother Raymond Terry, one of our construction managers,
assigned each person to a job. On a multi-million-dollar project,

there were lots of work to go around, and these men were willing to work, and they worked relentlessly, donating their time. When they came on the job, they had no experience in construction. So on the first day, they observed; and on the second, some started laying Sheetrock and did other related jobs. Their help was godsent. It was a time when funds were very low; but despite the funds, they stayed with us for approximately four months.

Business leaders in the community also helped. For example, God must have spoken to the hearts of Nassau County Court. We had not sought their help, but they sent men and women volunteers who did skilled work and cleaned the jobsite. Ms. Evelyn Core and Mr. Mimi Fezzini of Jamaica Ash, a community-oriented business, donated free dumpsters to cart away the garbage and made financial contributions. Bill Wiser and the late Phyllis Kreitman made financial contributions for the construction, and they continued their financial support to the church. My thanks and appreciation go to all of them.

My sincere gratitude goes to those who were there from the very inception of the new construction, including Reverend Euton and Sister Sylvia Watson, Sister Pauline Watson, Rev. Annette Ridley and Deacon Dudley Ridley, Mother Isoline and Cecil Simmonds, Deacon Harlan and Dr. Marie Ramsay, Sister Claudine Jessamy, Sister Sonia Creary, Minister Milton and Cordelia Martin, Sister Olive Foskey, Brother Raymond and Rose Terry, Rev. Renecca and Rev. Arthur Pinnock, Rev. Philman and Alceta Moulton, Brother and Sister Othneil Brown, Rev. Dr. Jefferson Bannister, his wife Cynthia and his congregation—Grace Church of God. My heartfelt thanks also to all the pastors and leaders of the Eastern New York General and Ministerial Assemblies for their prayers and generous support under the presiding leadership of the same Rev. Jefferson Bannister. There was a time we came to a crossroad and predicament as to how to pay to place the roof on the building. Rev Jefferson Bannister, President of the Eastern NY General Assembly and Ministerial Assembly, called a meeting and they came through with $20,000 dollars to purchase the materials for the roof. My gratefulness goes also to so many other persons who supported us with their prayers, their time, their talents, and their treasures in the form of loans and/or monetary contributions.

We never know where life's journey will take us or who will help us along the way. Nonetheless, if we stay in God's will, He will make possible what may seem impossible. As an example, the construction cost was over three million dollars ($3,000,000). Thanks be to God, City National Bank had found favor with us and gave us a loan of seven hundred thousand dollars ($700.000), with a promise to lend us another three hundred thousand dollars ($300,000), as the construction progressed. When the $700,000 they loaned us was exhausted, *neither we nor the bank knew where the remaining money would be coming from to finish the job, if they loan us the extra $300,000.* Therefore, they were reluctant to make good on their promise.

However, God was with us, considering that banks are not willing to give a partial construction loan without knowing where the rest of the money will be coming from to complete the job. I was told by the bank manager that they never like to see their money tied up in unfinished construction.

When the one million dollars plus our $350,000 were exhausted, I felt like Moses standing at the Red Sea, not knowing how to cross over.

However, I heard the Lord's voice from deep in my spirit: "Haven't I blessed you?"

I said, "Yes, Lord."

Then I heard Him say, "Refinance your house and loan the money to the church to complete the construction."

I relayed my conviction to my wife. We discussed it and prayed to the Lord and told the members of our decision. They were very receptive, and we did as the Lord commanded. What a joy it was to be able to release what in fact belongs to the Lord and complete the work that He had started.

At the time of our loan, Rev. Ben Chambers of the Rosedale Church of God and his congregation had decided to worship with us. His church had recently burnt out and they brought from their Church's settlement $160,000 including balance in treasury, and gave it to the Church. Rev. Dr. Jefferson Bannister and Grace Church of

God came through with $100,000 dollars to help in the completion of the construction. Their generosity to us was immeasurable. With the additional funds, the new church building was completed by June 2010.

My God never ceases to amaze me with the way He does things. He wanted the church to be built by faith and total trust in Him, not with the ready cash we had lost through the closure of the Church Extension of the Church of God, Anderson, Indiana. He was proving to us that He is God and His glory must shine forth.

However, after the building was completed, the village board and the bank that loaned us the money for construction notified us that we were in default because of incompletion of the proposed plans. The parking lot needed to be asphalted, the property had to be fenced, and shrubberies planted around its perimeter. These requirements were necessary before the restrictions would be lifted and the certificate of occupancy granted. We had no money to complete those tasks. The parking lot would cost seventy thousand dollars ($70,000). We knew only one source to draw from: prayer.

One dark and drizzly Monday morning, we met at the church for prayer and were discussing these latest challenges, asking God to send His help. While we were praying, help was already on the way. I called Assistant Pastor Rev. and Sister Watson into my office. Suddenly, the front door opened, and Rev. Jefferson Bannister[3] and two other church members from Grace of God entered. He came up to me, said, "Good morning," and handed me an envelope.

Without knowing what was in it, I said, "Thank you," and raised it up toward heaven and gave thanks to God.

I was overwhelmed and did not open it until Pastor Watson said, "Pastor, please open the envelope."

When I did, it was for thirty thousand dollars, exactly what was needed for the down payment on the parking lot. Pastor Bannister then said, "It's not a loan. It's a gift."

God had heard our prayers and sent three people in the form of angels to supply our needs. God had placed Pastor Bannister to lead the Eastern NY General Assembly during our time of building needs. The Assembly ran its own Capital Campaign that generated thousands of dollars to support major projects that would also mutually meet needs of the assembly. One such need was assembly space during conventions. The next Monday, I went to a meeting of the Eastern New York General Assembly where other pastors pledged to pay off the remaining forty thousand dollars for the parking lot within one year. They did so *in ten months*. In the meantime, we raised the necessary funds to purchase and install the fence and shrubberies. We paused to give God thanks for a very rewarding journey. We knew that God was in all our undertakings. One thing I know is that God will finish what He has started. Completion of the new edifice has enabled us to expand our food and clothing program to meet the needs of the less fortunate.

While going through this amazing journey toward completion of the construction and simultaneously pastoring, I realized that I needed to consider carefully and prayerfully how best to transfer administrative skills I had learned as a sole proprietor of my own business to the church setting. The church required responsibilities and skills new to me: clarity of mission, leadership, personnel staffing, financial management, and upkeep of the church.

---

[3] Pastor of Grace Church of God, Brooklyn, New York.

Through study and experience, I learned what I believe are important aspects of pastoring. For example, I always go into a church meeting well "prayed up" and with an open mind. I try to anticipate the opinions likely to be expressed. As a leader, I do not depend only on others to interpret what is communicated. I always listen and try to discern hidden messages and am always ready to dialogue. An administrative pastor must be adequately prepared when addressing meetings from a secular or religious perspective. As an authoritative person, he/she must always lead by example and should live a life above reproach. An administrative pastor is the CEO of the corporation, and every eye is on his leadership. He/she must seek God's guidance in every aspect of the pastorate. Our job is not a showpiece, but we must lead with love and humility. However, humility does not mean weakness; within humility, there is assertiveness.

The combination of my administrative experience and my strong Christian faith has helped me to enable many people to excel in their secular roles as well as mentored disciples to be administrative servants of the Lord Jesus Christ. When mentored, administrative servants carry out the duties assigned to them with distinction. I have encouraged leaders to lead by example and live a life above reproach because in life's journey, one never knows the success, failure, or challenges that lie ahead.

3

CHAPTER

Ministry Advocacy: National and International

J esus had breakfast by the sea with his disciples:

So when they had dined, Jesus said to Simon Peter, Simon, son of Jonas, lovest thou me more than these? Jesus and feeding his sheep: He said unto him, Yea, Lord; thou knowest that I love thee. He said unto him feed my lambs. He saith to him again the second time, Simon, son of Jonas, "lovest, thou me? He said unto him, Yea, Lord; thou knowest that I love thee. He said unto him feed my sheep." (St. John 21: 15, 16, TCRB)

I have been an activist inside and outside of my community. For fifteen years, I was vice president for the Eastern New York General Assembly of the Church of God in New York, under the leadership of the late Rev. Dr. John Bethea, Rev. Dr. Arthur Davenport, and Rev. Dr. Jefferson Bannister. I served as treasurer and vice president for the Westbury Improvement Corporation for four years.

For fifteen years, I have been serving as vice president for Unified New Castle (UNC), which was commended by former secretary of state Hillary Clinton and other dignitaries for their community development initiatives. UNC oversees the building of houses, commercial and retail stores, a recreational center for youth and seniors and feeding and clothing programs. I love to serve my local community, but I also look beyond. I want to share one example that might spark your interest and passion to consider the plight of the poor and in need and hopefully act upon that mission interest.

About forty years ago, I was approached by a deacon from another church, asking if I would be interested in feeding the needy. I said yes. He took me to a food bank and introduced me to the person in charge. After some discussion, the director assigned me to be one of the distributing agents in my community. I believe that feeding and clothing the needy is a mandate of Jesus and one of the greatest missions of the church, so this assignment further sparked my passion.

Since that day, I have been involved with the distribution of food and clothing to the needy in our community, surrounding areas, and the metropolitan city. Our church provides a nutritious breakfast every Sunday morning for Sunday school students. Twice monthly, we distribute food and clothing to the needy, and we distribute food baskets at Thanksgiving and Christmas. For many years, we had an annual Community Outreach Day, which included an old-fashioned barbecue, health forum, and other workshops.

I was not involved in this area until I was introduced to the food bank distributor. I had heard about it but never had hands-on experience, and I had not studied the subject. I learned through trial and error from the experiences of others. One of my experiences came on a mission to the island of Jamaica, my own homeland.

In 2009, Hurricane Gilbert devastated the island. Jamaicans nicknamed it "Rufus" because the roofs on almost all the houses and business places were ripped off by the hurricane's voracity. I purposed in my heart that I would take a delegation to go and help, not knowing what would befall us. However, before I did so, I prayed to the Lord to give me a word, and He gave me Psalm 41:1–2: "Blessed is he that considereth the poor: Jehovah will deliver him in the day of evil. Jehovah will preserve him, and keep him alive, and he shall be blessed upon the earth" (ASV). I took a delegation of missionaries to distribute food, clothing, medical supplies, zinc, and other amenities in two containers, one twenty-foot and the other forty-foot. This was a mission of mercy to help in a devastating disaster.

When we arrived on the island three weeks after the hurricane, we found that some of the goods had been stolen from the containers, and that we had misunderstood the fees for storage space. The storage facility's owner threatened seizure or impoundment of the containers if we could not pay the fees. We paid the fees. The next day, we hired trucks and dispatched them to different parts of the island.

The disaster was of biblical proportions. Streets were washed away, there was no electricity, mudslides were everywhere, uprooted trees blocked many of the minor and major roads, water supplies were destroyed, and drinking soda and coconut water for most of the time was unthinkable. We were the first to reach some of the more desolate communities to distribute supplies and share the Gospel with the people. The people told us that they were waiting for government help that never arrived. We had local people set up the locations and distribute the food supplies. Sadly, many were not trustworthy. They were hiding supplies for their friends and relatives while desperately needy people were waiting to be served.

We had to change how the distribution was conducted and provide strict supervision to others who were helping. Still, we were able to feed and clothe hundreds of needy people. We supplied them with blankets and zinc for their roofs and gave much-needed medical supplies to the local pharmacy.

When embarking on a big project like shipping two large containers to another country or island, there are definite risk factors. Mistakes will happen, and lessons can be learned. The first mistake that I made was not getting the proper information in writing about the storage facility, the costs involved, and the trustworthiness of the facility. The lesson was that one should not accept verbal agreements, even from one's best friend. The other mistake I made was not providing strict supervision over distribution of the supplies.

In times of emergency, one must react to accommodate the situation. In this case, I did not have time to seek out mentors and did not know anyone who had been on such a mission. Our delegation became "self-mentored" and learned through trial and error.

However, we were well "prayed up" before going on the journey, and I had no doubt that God was our best mentor. He guided and helped us to make good decisions when necessary. I was over-whelmed with emotion when I saw the lack of government help, the need of the people, and the suffering of those who had no roofs on their houses; the business places destroyed; their crops and livestock destroyed; and their water supplies contaminated. It was truly a dev-astating scene.

That was our first and last foreign mission of that magnitude, and it was a memorable one, but my involvement in distributing food and clothing to the needy at home and abroad continues. I send barrels to Haiti, Africa, and Jamaica. Feeding and clothing people in difficult situations such as hurricanes and other natural disasters, loss of jobs, and illness. These situations heighten my emotions and strengthen my resolve to help. I have preached and taught on many subjects of substance, but missionary work is very dear to my heart.

So much of what Jesus did when He came on His mission to earth was helping people in need and whose sins had separated them from Him. My personal philosophy is to follow Jesus's example, to carry out His mission to our fellow human beings. When the late Dr. Martin Luther King was on his mission for peace, equality, and justice for all, he often cited these lines:

> If I can help somebody as I pass along,
> if I can cheer somebody with a song,
> if I can show somebody he's traveling wrong,
> then my living will not be in vain.
> If I can do my duty as a Christian ought,
> then my living will not be in vain.[4]

And he hoped when he died: "I want you to be able to say that day at my funeral, I did try to feed the hungry. I want you to say that day that I did try in my life to clothe those who were naked."[5]

Dr. Martin Luther King was clearly on a mission of mercy for humanity. Like Jesus and Dr. King, this is what God is calling upon

---

[4] Alma Irene Bazel Androzzo, "If I Can Help Somebody" (1945).
[5] Martin Luther King Jr., "The Drum Major Instinct" (1968).

all believers to do. Life is a journey; and when this life ends, our journey and service to humanity also end. While we are alive and well, we must carry out Jesus's mission to feed and clothe the needy and help those who are sick and/or mentally challenged in our community and beyond.

4
CHAPTER

DEPRESSION AND ANXIETY: AN EXERCISE

Without passion or keen spiritual clarity, those who are
depressed find it nearly impossible to maintain a vision for
the things that are important. There is nothing emerging
from their haze of despair to capture their attention.

—Edward T. Welch, Trinity Online Learning
Center: BC330/504/820Webinar/6/15/15?

W hen I consider my early schooling, I must acknowledge that my
life's journey has taken me to places in learning that far exceeded my
expectations. In this section, I am sharing a hypothetical counseling
exercise to encourage those who might have a heart for counseling
especially those experiencing depression and anxiety. To develop this
narrative, I have drawn upon my readings in this area, used a set of
guiding questions posed by Prof. Elbert. E. Elliot, provost/vice president of academic affairs, Trinity College of the Bible and Theological
Seminary.

*What strategy would you employ in your request to gain accurate
and relevant data that you must gather if you are to provide relevant and
effective direction for Ben? Be sure to state specific method and assessments
that you would utilize, including the questions that you might pose.*

Ben came to Grace Counseling Center where I served as a counselor, and he was assigned to me. The first thing I did was gather as much intake data that was available. From this, I learned that he came only because his wife insisted. I would first introduce myself to Ben and try to determine his reason for being here. When he comes in, I would note my first impression of him; for example, if he was unkempt or seemed to be reluctant. Then I would introduce myself and try to put him at ease. I would ask him why he has come in and listen carefully, perhaps ask a few clarification questions to show my concern and compassion. Establishing such an approach hopefully would help build our relationship and assure him that counseling is worth trying.

In this case, the counselee never made eye contact and kept his arms crossed across his chest. After reviewing all the data about Ben, it appeared that he had multiple issues that needed God-given wisdom and understanding for him to recover from his depression. As Collins has stated:

> Depressed people are often private, non-verbal, poorly motivated, pessimistic, and characterized by a resigned "what's-the-use?" attitude. The counselor, therefore, must reach out verbally so that he or she might share with other counselees. Sharing of facts on how depression affects people, patiently encouraging the counselee to talk, (but not pushing them), asking questions, giving periodic compliments and gentle sharing of scripture (without preaching) can all be helpful.[6]

Wright[7] has also suggested the importance of active listening, so that the depressed person might be more willing to and release and share more about his/her pain and hurt. Knowing some of Ben's

---

[6] Garry H. Collins, PhD, (1988), Christian Counseling: A Comprehensive Guide, revised edition: p.111, Zondervan Bible Publishers, U.S.A.

[7] H. Norman Wright, *Crisis Counseling* (Regal Books, 1993), 111.

history, for example, I would ask him to further elaborate on what brought him to this juncture and if he had ever had counseling before. If he said yes, I would ask him why he discontinued. At the end of our session, I would ask him if he had any thoughts or concerns after this first session. If he seemed to hesitate, I would give him some time and try to assure him that his response could be either positive or negative. Then I would suggest our next steps and try to confirm his agreement.

What actions and attitudes in Ben's life might have a negative impact on you to remain compassionate and objective in your counseling work with him? State how these factors might impact you and the approach you would take to make certain that your effectiveness is not minimized.

Ben is not able to make eye contact with me; he is withdrawn, has difficulty recalling some facts about his life, and keeps his arms crossed on his chest. In such a situation, he may not share valuable information with me. All these factors could have a negative impact on my remaining compassionate and objective or to keep trying. Therefore, I would continue to encourage him by praising his attending a community college even though he couldn't continue at the time. I would assure him that all of us can improve in some way, and that I thought he could be benefited from a different learning center where he could pursue a new trade. Checking always to see his reaction and response, I would further point him to a scripture where Jesus encouraged people, especially,

> Come unto me all who are weary and heavy laden, and I will give you rest. Take my yoke upon you, and lean on me; for I am gentle and humble in heart, and you shall find rest for your soul. For my yoke is easy, and my burden is light. (Matthew 11:28–30, TCRB)

Encouraging Ben should provide him some hope in the possibility of change and encourage me to keep on trying.

Based on the facts presented in the narrative, what concerns need to be confronted in Ben's thoughts and actions? State the approach you would utilize in this phase of your counseling work.

Depression is often cited as a cause of feelings of shame for the kind of behaviors exhibited by Ben, and we often hear it said that one way to change our feelings is to change our thoughts. Through the initial information about Ben and our communications so far, it has become clear that he might be seeking to develop a better and closer relationship with God. In Ben's case, in childhood, he apparently did not have an intimate relationship with his earthly father and mother and, therefore, did not understand that God, his heavenly Father, accepted him just as he is. He would be assured that God is yearning for intimacy with him and even looking to establish a relationship with him. That makes him very special: "For the eyes of the LORD run to and fro through the whole earth to show himself strong in the behalf of them whose heart is perfect towards him" (2 Chronicles 16:9, KJV).

I would encourage Ben to build a closeness to God through prayer and reading the Word of God, because God "wilt keep him in perfect peace, whose mind is stayed on [God]" (Isaiah 26:3, KJV).

Depression often suggests a person's lack of internal peace, and one way to gain that peace is to keep one's mind on God. Welch, for example, has asserted that spiritual concerns should be confronted in depressed persons:

> Without passion or keen spiritual clarity, those who are depressed find it nearly impossible to maintain a vision for the things that are important. There is nothing emerging from their haze of despair to capture their attention.[8]

Ben can be encouraged and reassured that if he really learns to trust and depend on God, He can relieve his fears and doubts. Scripture and the experiences of other depressed persons remind us

---

[8] Welch, 202.

that "the steps of a good [person] are ordered by the Lord, and he delighted in his way. Though he falls, he shall not be utterly cast down, for the Lord upholds them with His hand" (Psalm 37:23–24, AMP), and "He sent from above, He took me; He drew me out of great waters" (Psalm 18:16, NKJV).

God watches out for all of us, including Ben. He loves him beyond what he can comprehend. He is very concerned when he falls, and He wants to help us get up. He will protect us if we will trust Him to order our steps.

Ben appears to have some material needs as well. I would urge him to take care of his personal appearance. I also would recommend that he explore a local church or other facilities in his area that offer health and other social services such as rehabilitation help, support groups, and/or food pantries. Referral to services in his location might further meet his needs, and I would recommend some and ask him to let me know what happens.

What specific truths might you share with Ben to enable him to realize that there is hope for him? Include a selection of biblical passages that you would employ and your rationale for the use of each text.

Here are the primary and specific truths that I would share with Ben for him to realize that there is hope for him. I would tell him that depression is real, and it affects the old as well as the young, the rich and the poor, and of whatever ethnicity. But the Word of God states that anxiety in the heart of a person causes depression, "but a good word makes it glad" (Proverbs 12:25, NKJV).

I would emphasize to him that when a person is discouraged, unmotivated, and bored with life, he/she often also has self-esteem, self-pity, and a lack of self-confidence, and therefore prefers to stay away from other people. Social contact may be too demanding, and the depressed person may not feel like communicating, instead daydreaming and/or escaping into the world of television.[9] I would give an example of King David in the scripture. Television did not exist during David's time, yet he was still depressed. However, he drew from the reservoir of God's Word, which was hidden in his heart. For

---

9   Collins, 110.

that reason, he could say, "Why are you cast down, O my soul?" but also conclude with "hope in God for I shall yet praise him, who *is* the help of my countenance and my God" (Psalm 43:5, NKJV).

There are so many other scriptures that can help, including Philippians 4:13 and Romans 12:2. Hopefully Ben would ask for other references, which I would also provide.

What two homework assignments might you develop for Ben over the course of providing counseling to him? Provide clear directions as to how you might make the assignments and explain what you consider to be the value of each assignment.

Reassurance is of utmost importance to Ben, so I would suggest homework assignments that could keep on encouraging him.

1. I would ask Ben to develop a habit of reading scriptures daily that can offer comfort, reassurance, and discipline. I would further suggest that he ask specific family members to call him at specific times for brief conversation or encouragement and offering scripture verses such as Isaiah 40:28–31 or Philippians 4:4–9. I would specify that he provide these and/or other verses in writing, give them to the family member, and read them aloud together.

2. Exercise is an active approach to daily living for all and a good antidote to depression. Dr. Otto Appenzeller of the University of New Mexico has found that the nervous system releases hormones called catecholamines during marathon running, increasing in all marathon runners to six hundred percent above normal.[10] It has also been found that hormones are low in depressed persons; therefore, the connection between running and release of those could be generalized to recommend at least moderate forms of exercise.[11]

---

[10] H. Norman Wright, Crisis Counseling
Regal Books, A Division of Gospel Light
Ventura, California USA.
Publish in the USA: 1993
[11] Wright, 111–115.

Since Ben seems to shy away from close human contact, I would also encourage him to find at least one person (family member, neighbor, friend) in whom he can confide and to whom he can vent his feelings, negative or positive. Together, they could go over his daily activities, check his accomplishments, and reward himself with a "Yes!" This would help him establish an important relationship of trust and support throughout his depressive state and hopefully beyond.

Equipped with the combination of scriptures and other techniques, Ben can hopefully face the stubborn darkness of depression and anxiety and be encouraged by the Word of God, knowing that joy is within reach.

Reader, I hope that as you have journeyed with me through this narrative, your heart will be inspired to help the downtrodden and depressed.

5
CHAPTER

WHY I HAVE WRITTEN MY STORY

I am writing my story to help motivate persons who might be at the point of despair and feel like giving up. One must believe in one's God-given potential and remember that there is hope. Have a vision and work that vision out, then just watch it unfold. Never surround yourself with negative people who can discourage you and bring you down to their level. Try to think positively even when things are not going the way you would like and try to envision a brighter outcome. When others rule you out as a "duffer," prove them wrong and don't give up because your future is in God's hand, not theirs, and not yours. You are a star because you were made in the amalgamated image of our Lord Jesus Christ.

The Rev. Jessie Jackson once said, "Although you were born in the ghetto, the ghetto was not born in you." He was saying that you can rise above your situation. Remember, life is a journey; and with God's help, there are endless possibilities. When it is over, there is no return to make amends. God did not call us to live a depressed and depraved life. He called us to live to our fullest potential, although sometimes we are our biggest enemies. We are afraid to step out by faith because we are so afraid of what other people will think of us.

I am not proud to say that I was an elementary school dropout and was written off as a "duffer." But although I was labeled, I did not give up. I went on to earn my high school diploma, a bachelor's, and a master's degree.

Still, I would never encourage a young person to neglect or stop attending school. There are those who procrastinate and put off what might be accomplished now. In their young minds, they think that they will later be smarter. I say, "Bad choice." That can lead to regretting the past. I found that when one does not complete the fundamentals of elementary education, it's very hard to recoup. I therefore encourage all young people to stay in school, listen to your parents and teachers, and you will never regret it. As Apostle Paul exhorts in Ephesians:

> Children, obey your parents in the Lord, for this is right: Honor your father and your mother, which is the first commandment with promise, that it may be well with you and you may live long on the earth. (6:1–3, TCRB)

This journey has not always been easy, but I do not regret the leading of the Lord in my life. He has blessed me with gifts and resources that far surpassed my expectations. The gifts of teaching, preaching, counseling, and entrepreneurship have all helped me to train others to be successful in religious or secular settings. I believe I have had an impact on many other lives along this journey. I fervently pray that they too will be rewarded by having an impact on others for the good of humanity and for the glory of our Lord Jesus Christ.

APPENDIX

PAST AND PRESENT LEADERS OF THE CHURCH AND THEIR POSITIONS

1. Sis. Sylvia Watson: first secretary/Sunday school teacher
2. Rev. Nomey Peynado: first Christian education director/assistant secretary/Sunday school teacher
3. Sis. Hortense Dawkins: first organist/fund-raiser
4. Sis. Cordelia Martin: organist/treasurer
5. Deacon Adam Dawkins: first treasurer/bus driver
6. Rev. Annette Ridley: youth pastor/trustees chair
7. Bro. Joe Redfearn: first ushers' president
8. Sis. Olga Donaldson: ushers' president
9. Bro Calvin Morris: usher/bus driver
10. Sis. Viola Morris: usher
11. Sis. Mavis Douglas: ushers' president/entertainment committee
12. Sis. Olive Foskey: assistant organist/fund-raiser
13. Sis. Sonia Creary: secretary/Sunday school teacher
14. Sis. Claudine Jessamy: treasurer/Sunday school teacher/choir member
15. Sis. Henrietta Redfearn: Sunday school superintendent/teacher
16. Bro. Raymond Terry: trustee chair/church builder
17. Rev. Philmon Moulton: trustee
18. Sis. Loriann Pommells: youth president
19. Rev. Hermine Campbell: nursing home ministry

20. Min. Alceta Moulton: Christian education director
21. Deaconess Edna McQueen: nursing home ministry
22. Deacon George McKen: vocalist/chairman of the deacon board
23. Deaconess Hyacinth McKen: secretary/women's connection/resource person
24. Sis. Kerry Woodhouse: secretary
25. Bro. Eagan William: bus driver
26. Bro. Locksley Pommells: substitute bus driver
27. Rev. Euton Watson: assistant pastor/assistant bus driver
28. Deacon Harlan Ramsay: chairman of the deacon board
29. Rev Dr. Marie Ramsay: teacher/preacher
30. Sis. Marion Peynado: Sunday school superintendent/teacher/assistant secretary

I must introduce some of those whom I have met on this journey and were licensed and ordained under my leadership.

1. Rev. Nomey Peynado
2. Rev. Renecca Pinnock
3. Min. Milford Martin
4. Rev. Hermine Campbell
5. Rev. Dr. Marie Ramsay
6. Rev. Philmon Moulton
7. Min. Alcita Moulton
8. Rev. Dr. Dwayne Dawkins
9. Min. Earl Noble
10. And several other deacons and deaconesses

Rev. Michael Peynado and his wife Nomey Peynado

ABOUT THE AUTHOR

Rev. Michael Peynado is the senior pastor of the Westbury Divine Church of God, located at 911 Brush Hollow Road, Westbury New York 11590, where he has been serving for forty one years.

Rev. Peynado holds a Bachelor's degree in Theology from Southern California School of Ministry, New York Campus, also a Master's degree from Trinity College of the Bible and Theological Seminary, where he focused on counseling. Rev. Mike, as he is so fondly called, has the ability to motivate people by encouraging them to reach their fullest potential, and not to succumb to discouragement or negative influence.

Rev. Peynado is very much involved in his community with other ministers, community leaders and who-ever is interested in the wellbeing and development of the community. He is also working with the Eastern New York General Assembly of the Church of God, which consists of twenty four churches. In that capacity he helps to interview and counsel those candidates who will be licensed and ordained for ministry.

He has proven to be a Pastor of outstanding character. His God given wisdom, and compassion in dealing with the downtrodden and oppressed is to be commended. Together, Rev. Peynado and his wife Nomey has three children, five grandchildren and two great grandchildren.

CPSIA information can be obtained
at www.ICGtesting.com
Printed in the USA
LVHW020025310520
656910LV00006B/649